THE LITTLE BOOK OF
BORIS

Published by Orange Hippo!
20 Mortimer Street
London W1T 3JW

ISBN 978-1-91161-029-8

Editorial: Ross Hamilton, Victoria Godden
Project Manager: Russell Porter
Design: Tony Seddon
Production: Jessica Arvidsson

A CIP catalogue for this book is available from the British Library

Printed in Dubai

10 9 8 7 6 5 4 3 2 1

Jacket cover photograph: Jeff J Mitchell/Getty Images

THE LITTLE BOOK OF

BORIS

IN HIS OWN WORDS

CONTENTS

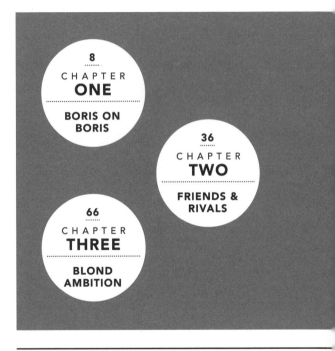

INTRODUCTION

Few, if any, politicians are as innately quotable as Alexander Boris de Pfeffel Johnson. Or just "Boris", as he is almost universally known.

For more than 25 years, Boris has been a fixture of British politics, media and pop culture. His rise, though often far from smooth, has seen him progress from Eton hellraiser and journalist provocateur to Conservative MP, Mayor of London and – eventually – Prime Minister of the United Kingdom. Throughout the highs and lows (often, it must be said, of his own making), Boris has never shied away from the spotlight. Whether waxing lyrical in his newspaper columns, giving an impromptu interview or going off-script at a live event, he has a knack for improvisation that has led to him delivering some of the most memorable quotes of recent times.

Boris has mastered a particular brand of the English language that is unique to him, and over the years has turned his attention to all manner of worldly topics. He has bellowed arcane insults at rivals and naysayers, made decidedly undiplomatic comments about world leaders, and extolled the virtues of everything from drugs to beach volleyball. No matter the subject, his words rarely fail to provoke a response, whether it's laughter, fury, embarrassment or bemusement.

This *Little Book of Boris* contains many of his 'greatest hits' and plenty of his more 'problematic' quotes besides – from Brexit and benefits to Donald Trump and Jeremy Corbyn. For every pearl of wisdom, there's a cringeworthy clanger to match it, but then that's what makes Boris, well, Boris. Whether you admire him, despise him, or land somewhere in between, you'll find plenty of statements here at which to chortle, tut, or simply raise your eyebrows in astonishment.

Read on.

CHAPTER
ONE

BORIS ON BORIS

66

I have as much chance of becoming Prime Minister as of being decapitated by a frisbee.

On future plans, 2003

99

I'm having Sunday lunch with my family. I'm vigorously campaigning, inculcating my children in the benefits of a Tory government. "

On canvassing, The Guardian,
11 April 2005

66

If sometimes... I use phrases and language which have caused offence, I, of course, am sorry for the offence I have caused. But I will continue to speak as directly as I can because that is what I think the British public want.

99

On straight-talking, Conservative leadership campaign launch, 12 June 2019

My ambition silicon chip has been programmed to try to scramble up this *cursus honorum*, this ladder of things.

On ambition, Desert Island Discs,
30 October 2005

66

Some readers will no doubt say
that a devil is inside me; and
though my faith is a bit like Magic
FM in the Chilterns, in that the
signal comes and goes, I can
only hope that isn't so.

99

On spirituality, Daily Telegraph,
4 March 2004

66

I mildly sandpapered something somebody said.

On making up a quote, BBC, 24 March 2013

99

66

Face it: it's all your own
fat fault.

On being overweight, Daily Telegraph,
27 May 2004

99

66

Never in my life did I think I would
be congratulated by Mick Jagger
for achieving anything.

99

On becoming Mayor of London,
New York Times Magazine, *1 June 2012*

My friends, as I have discovered myself, there are no disasters, only opportunities. And, indeed, opportunities for fresh disasters.

On being fired by Michael Howard, Daily Telegraph, *2 December 2004*

If we judged everybody by the
stupid, unguarded things they
blurt out to their nearest and
dearest, then we wouldn't ever
get anywhere.

On private conversations, 29 April 2010

"

I love tennis with a passion. I challenged Boris Becker to a match once and he said he was up for it but he never called back. I bet I could make him run around. **"**

On tennis, Daily Express, *21 March 2005*

66

My speaking style was criticised by no less an authority than Arnold Schwarzenegger. It was a low moment, my friends, to have my rhetorical skills denounced by a monosyllabic Austrian cyborg. **99**

Conservative Party conference,
28 September 2008

66

I don't know what a pint of milk costs. So what?

99

On buying groceries, BBC,
30 September 2013

66

I believe I am best placed to lift
this party, beat Jeremy Corbyn and
excite people about conservatism
and conservative values.

99

*On his candidacy for leadership of
the Conservative Party, 4 June 2019*

We can all spend an awfully long time going over lots of stuff that I've written over the last 30 years… all of which in my view have been taken out of context, but never mind…

On being misquoted, 19 July 2016

66

I'm afraid that there is such a rich thesaurus now of things that I have said that have been one way or another, through what alchemy I do not know, somehow misconstrued that it would take me too long to engage in a full global itinerary of apology to all concerned. 99

On past mistakes, 19 July 2016

66

Some people play the piano, some do Sudoku, some watch television, some people go out to dinner parties. I write books. **99**

On his literary skills, New York Times Magazine, *1 June 2012*

66

I have not been more robust towards female rather than male assembly members and I do not believe I have been remotely sexist.

99

On sexism, The Guardian, *22 April 2012*

66

I think I was once given cocaine
but I sneezed so it didn't go up
my nose. In fact, I may have
been doing icing sugar.

99

On drugs, Have I Got News For You, *2005*

66

I have not had an affair with Petronella. It is complete balderdash. It is an inverted pyramid of piffle. It is all completely untrue and ludicrous conjecture. I am amazed people can write this drivel.

99

On an alleged affair with Petronella Wyatt, Mail on Sunday, *7 November 2004*

66

I advise you all very strongly – go for a run, get some exercise, and have a beautiful day.

99

In response to questions about an alleged affair, 15 November 2004

“

I was just chucking these rocks over the garden wall, and I'd listen to this amazing crash from the greenhouse, next door, over in England.

"

On being Brussels correspondent for the Telegraph, Desert Island Discs, October 2005

.

66

Everything I wrote from Brussels was having this amazing, explosive effect on the Tory Party, and it really gave me this, I suppose, rather weird sense of, of power.

99

On being Brussels correspondent for the Telegraph, Desert Island Discs, October 2005

66

I cannot swear I have always observed the speed limit of 70mph.

On whether he had ever done anything illegal, 12 June 2019

Dark forces dragged me away from the keyboard, swirling forces of irresistible intensity and power.

On missing deadlines, Sunday Times, *16 July 2000*

66

My chances of being PM are about as good as the chances of finding Elvis on Mars, or my being reincarnated as an olive.

99

On being Prime Minister, June 2004

CHAPTER
TWO

FRIENDS
& RIVALS

66

Despite looking a bit like Dobby
the House Elf, he is a ruthless and
manipulative tyrant.

99

*On Russian President Vladimir Putin,
the Telegraph, 7 December 2015*

If he can fix North Korea and if he can fix the Iran nuclear deal then I don't see why he is any less of a candidate for the Nobel Peace Prize than Barack Obama, who got it before he even did anything.

On Donald Trump's Nobel Prize chances,
Sky News, 7 May 2018

66

We are confident in our story
and will be fighting this all the
way. I am very sorry that Alastair
Campbell has taken this decision
but I can see that he got his tits
in the wringer.

99

In defence of a Spectator *article,*
The Herald, *24 April 2002*

66

[He's] a rather engaging geezer.

On Nigel Farage, the Telegraph,
29 April 2013

99

"

I forgot that to rely on a train, in Blair's Britain, is to engage in a crapshoot with the devil.

"

On commuting, Daily Telegraph, *3 July 2003*

It was never nicked during all my time as mayor and I used to chain it up across the whole city. Barely had Sadiq Khan's reign begun before it was nicked.

On his missing bike, "Bikey",
15 July 2019

66

What has the BBC come to?
Toilets, that's what.

99

Headline for his column in the Telegraph,
14 March 2002

What a sharp-elbowed thrusting and basically repellent lot we were. Always bragging and shafting each other. And in a way we still are.

On his Oxford contemporaries,
The Spectator, *25 October 2006*

66

Only a socialist could do that to his brother, only a socialist could regard familial ties as being so trivial as to shaft his own brother... I mean, unbelievable.

99

On Ed and David Miliband,
The Australian, *2013*

66

He's lost the plot, people tell me.
He's drifting rudderless in the wide
Sargasso Sea of New Labour's
ideological vacuum.

99

On Tony Blair, Daily Telegraph,
29 April 2004

The President is a cross-eyed Texan warmonger, unelected, inarticulate, who epitomises the arrogance of American foreign policy.

On President George W. Bush,
The Spectator, *22 November 2003*

This is nothing less than a palace coup, effected by the Brownites, and it is possible only because Tony had run out of road.

On Gordon Brown becoming Prime Minister, Daily Telegraph, 21 June 2007

66

[The attack] was a sign that President Putin or the Russian state wanted to give to potential defectors in their own agencies: 'This is what happens to you if you decide to support a country with a different set of values. You can expect to be assassinated'.

99

On the Novichok attacks in Salisbury, 21 March 2018

❝
I think it is an emetic prospect, frankly, to think of Putin glorying in this sporting event. **❞**

On the prospect of the 2018 FIFA World Cup hosted by Russia, 21 March 2018

"

I'm backing David Cameron's campaign out of pure, cynical self-interest.

The Independent *conference diary,*
5 October 2005

Unlike the current occupant of the White House [George Bush], he has no difficulty in orally extemporising a series of grammatical English sentences, each containing a main verb.

On why he backed Barack Obama for US President, Daily Telegraph, *21 October 2008*

66

Howard is a dynamic performer on many levels. There you are. He sent me to Liverpool. Marvellous place. Howard was the most effective Home Secretary since Peel. Hang on, was Peel Home Secretary?

99

On Michael Howard, The Times,
19 April 2005

The Lib Dems are not just empty. They are a void within a vacuum surrounded by a vast inanition.

On the Liberal Democrats,
Daily Telegraph, *September 2003*

"

But here's old Ken – he's been crass, he's been insensitive and thuggish and brutal in his language – but I don't think actually if you read what he said, although it was extraordinary and rude, I don't think he was actually anti-Semitic.

"

On Ken Livingstone, Today,
BBC Radio 4, 17 February 2005

I can hardly condemn UKIP as a bunch of boss-eyed, foam-flecked Euro hysterics when I have been sometimes not far short of boss-eyed, foam-flecked hysteria myself.

On UKIP, 2004

❝

There was a young fellow
   from Ankara
Who was a terrific wankerer.
Till he sowed his wild oats
With the help of a goat
But he didn't even stop to
   thankera.

❞

On Turkish president Tayyip Erdoğan,
The Spectator, *18 May 2016*

It is just flipping unbelievable. He is a mixture of Harry Houdini and a greased piglet. He is barely human in his elusiveness. Nailing Blair is like trying to pin jelly to a wall.

On Tony Blair, Daily Telegraph,
29 January 2004

66

Hooray, I say. Bravo – and keep going.

On Bashar Al-Assad and the Syrian Civil War, The Telegraph, 27 March 2016

99

66

Old Man Howard, that Old Man Howard, he just keeps rolling, just keeps rolling.

On Michael Howard's longevity,
The Oxford Student, *2005*

99

"

She's got dyed blonde hair and pouty lips, and a steely blue stare, like a sadistic nurse in a mental hospital.

"

On Hillary Clinton,
Daily Telegraph, *1 November 2007*

66

Not only did I want Bush to win,
but we threw the entire weight of
The Spectator behind him.

99

On American elections,
Have I Got News For You, *2006*

66

Look, I wouldn't trust Harriet
Harman's political judgement.

99

*When told Harriet Harman believed
he had been elected Mayor of London,
BBC News, 2008*

66

As snow-jobs go, this beats
the Himalayas.

99

On the Hutton Report,
Daily Telegraph, *29 January 2004*

CHAPTER
THREE

BLOND AMBITION

"

I'm in politics to change things –
if possible, for the better.

"

On what motivates him,
The Spectator, *13 December 2014*

66

Will I throw my hat into the ring?
It depends on what kind of ring it
is and what kind of hat I have in
my hand.

99

In answer to a question from the
Oxford Mail on running for leadership of
the Conservative Party, 2016

66

This is about all of us. I am praying that we will wake from this sleepwalk to tragedy; and that the Scots vote no to divorce, and yes to Britain, the greatest political union ever.

99

On Scottish independence,
Daily Telegraph, *8 September 2014*

"

I think the risks that people see of terrorism are incredibly important but we are very confident we have got the right people on it and the risks have been minimised. **"**

On terrorism, 2012

66

In 1904, 20 per cent of journeys were made by bicycle in London. I want to see a figure like that again. If you can't turn the clock back to 1904, what's the point of being a Conservative?

99

On promoting cycling, 30 July 2010

We are willing to encourage the tech wizards and the shopkeepers and the taxi drivers and, yes, the bankers as well.

On investment, Conservative leadership campaign launch, 12 June 2019

66

I'm very attracted to it. I may be
diverting from Tory Party policy
here, but I don't care.

99

On 24-hour drinking legislation,
The Times, *30 April 2005*

66

No one can ignore the harshness of that competition or the inequality that it inevitably accentuates; and I am afraid that violent economic centrifuge is operating on human beings who are already very far from equal in raw ability, if not spiritual worth.

99

On inequality, The Guardian,
27 November 2013

London is a fantastic creator of jobs – but many of these jobs are going to people who don't originate in this country.

On London jobs, Daily Mail,
20 January 2012

What I worry about is that people are losing confidence, losing energy, losing enthusiasm, and there's a real opportunity to get them into work.

On employment, The Andrew Marr Show, *22 July, 2012*

66

Voting Tory will cause your
wife to have bigger breasts and
increase your chances of owning
a BMW M3.

99

On the campaign trail, 2005

"

My policy on cake is pro having it
and pro eating it.

On cake

"

66

I realise that there may be some confusion in my prescriptions between what I would do, what Maggie would do, and what the government is about to do or is indeed already doing... I don't think it much matters, because the three are likely to turn out to be one and the same.

99

On Thatcherism, 27 November 2013

We should be helping all those who can to join the ranks of the super-rich, and we should stop any bashing or moaning or preaching or bitching and simply give thanks for the prodigious sums of money that they are contributing to the tax revenues of this country.

On the rich, the Telegraph,
17 November 2013

66

Both the minimum wage and the
Social Charter would palpably
destroy jobs.

99

On financial policy,
Lend Me Your Ears, *2003*

I would like to thank first the vast multitudes who voted against me – and I have met quite a few in the last nine months, not all of them entirely polite. **"**

On becoming Mayor of London,
3 May 2008

66

The dreadful truth is that when people come to see their MP they have run out of better ideas.

99

On visiting your MP,
Daily Telegraph, *18 September 2003*

" It is easy to make promises – it is hard work to keep them. **"**

Talking about his first term as Mayor of London, 14 March 2012

66

What we hate, what we fear, is being ignored.

99

On an MP's greatest fear, 21 April 2005

66

Look the point is... er, what is the point? It is a tough job but somebody has got to do it. **99**

On being appointed Shadow Arts Minister, 7 May 2004

66

Nothing excites compassion, in friend and foe alike, as much as the sight of you ker-splonked on the Tarmac with your propeller buried six feet under.

99

On being sacked as Shadow Arts Minister, the Telegraph, *2 December 2004*

66
Government by a Scot is just
not conceivable in the current
constitutional context.

On a Scottish Prime Minister,
The Spectator, *9 April 2005*

66

I'm very keen on a Barnett formula which does justice to Barnet with one T. We can't just go on with a system that even Joel Barnett himself thinks is outdated.

99

On public expenditure, on a visit to Scotland during the Scottish independence vote, 19 September 2014

66

Whatever type of Wall's sausage is contrived by this great experiment, the dominant ingredient has got to be conservatism. The meat in the sausage has got to be Conservative, I would say. With plenty of bread and other bits and pieces.

99

On the possibility of a coalition government, BBC News, 2010

"

There is no point in wasting any more moral or mental energy in being jealous of the very rich. They are no happier than anyone else; they just have more money. We shouldn't bother ourselves about why they want all this money, or why it is nicer to have a bath with gold taps.

"

On jealousy, Daily Telegraph,
17 November 2013

If the ball came loose from the back of the scrum, which it won't of course, [becoming Prime Minister] would be a great, great thing to have a crack at.

On becoming Prime Minister, BBC, 26 March 2013

CHAPTER

FOUR

WHAT IN
THE WORLD?

66

Life isn't like coursework, baby.
It's one damn essay crisis after
another.

99

On the meaning of life,
Daily Telegraph, *12 May 2005*

66

I could not fail to disagree with you less.

99

Have I Got News For You,
December 2003

66

A pound spent in Croydon is of far more value to the country than a pound spent in Strathclyde. You will generate jobs in Strathclyde far more effectively if you invest in parts of London.

99

On Scotland, Huffington Post UK, *28 April 2012*

I said there were 250,000 French men and women in London and therefore I was the mayor of the sixth-biggest French city on Earth.

On London's French contingent, 2013

66

Yes, cannabis is dangerous, but no more than other perfectly legal drugs. It's time for a rethink, and the Tory Party – the funkiest, most jiving party on Earth – is where it's happening.

99

On drugs, Daily Telegraph, *12 July 2001*

66

The problem is not that we were once in charge, but that we are not in charge any more. **99**

On Africa, The Spectator,
2 February 2002

66

Exams work because they're scary.

Daily Telegraph, *12 May 2005*

66

A horse is a safer bet than the trains.

On the railway, Daily Telegraph, *3 July 2003*

99

66

It is possible to have a pretty good life and career being a leech and a parasite in the media world, gadding about from TV studio to TV studio, writing inconsequential pieces and having a good time.

99

On journalism, GQ magazine, July 2007

I remember the guts streaming, and the stag turds spilling out on to the grass from within the ventral cavity... this hunting is best for the deer.

On stag hunting, Lend Me Your Ears, *2003*

‟

It was jolly nice. But apparently it is very different these days. Much stronger. I've become very illiberal about it. I don't want my kids to take drugs.

„

On smoking cannabis, GQ magazine, June 2007

66

No one obeys the speed limit
except a motorised rickshaw.

99

On speed limits, Daily Telegraph,
21 June 2001

66

I don't believe that is necessarily any more dangerous than the many other risky things that people do with their free hands while driving – nose-picking, reading the paper, studying the A-Z, beating the children, and so on.

99

On using a mobile phone while driving, Daily Telegraph, *1 August 2002*

66

But if people want to swim in the Thames, if they want to take their lives into their own hands, then they should be able to do so with all the freedom and exhilaration of our woad-painted ancestors. **99**

On swimming in the City,
Daily Telegraph, *2 July 2012*

66

You may keep secrets from your friends, from your parents, your children, your doctor – even your personal trainer – but it takes real effort to conceal your thoughts from Google.

99

On privacy, UN General Assembly,
25 September 2019

It's great to be here, folks. It's absolutely wonderful to be here in Manchester, one of the few British cities I have yet to insult.

On Manchester, Conservative Party Conference, 5 October 2009

66

Chinese cultural influence is
virtually nil, and unlikely to
increase…

99

On China, Daily Telegraph,
1 September 2005

66

I don't see why people are so
snooty about Channel 5. It has
some respectable documentaries
about the Second World War.
It also devotes considerable
airtime to investigations into
lap-dancing and other related
and vital subjects.

99

On Channel 5, Daily Telegraph,
14 March 2002

66

The excitement is growing so much I think the Geiger counter of Olympo-mania is going to go zoink off the scale.

99

On the London 2012 Olympics
27 July 2012

66

If you tell me that the burka is oppressive, then I am with you. **99**

On burkas, Daily Telegraph, 5 August 2018

66.

In the future, voice connectivity will be in every room and almost every object: your mattress will monitor your nightmares; your fridge will beep for more cheese.

99

On technology, UN General Assembly, 25 September 2019

66

What will synthetic biology stand for – restoring our livers and our eyes with miracle regeneration of the tissues, like some fantastic hangover cure? Or will it bring terrifying limbless chickens to our tables?

99

On the future of food, UN General Assembly, 25 September 2019

66

They are like glistening wet otters frolicking.

99

*On women's beach volleyball at
the Olympics,* Daily Telegraph, *31 July 2012*

66

There is absolutely no one, apart from yourself, who can prevent you, in the middle of the night, from sneaking down to tidy up the edges of that hunk of cheese at the back of the fridge.

99

On midnight snacks,
Daily Telegraph, *27 May 2004*

66

Her silvery little skirt is so short it would be positively impolite not to have a quick dekko. **99**

On TV presenter
Catrina Skepper's legs, 1999

66

Had it been us staging the Games, I don't think we would necessarily have done the switcheroo with the girl with the braces.

99

On the 2008 Beijing Olympics,
The Guardian, *21 August 2008*

66

I'm a rugby player, really, and I knew I was going to get to him, and when he was about two yards away I just put my head down. There was no malice. I was going for the ball with my head, which I understand is a legitimate move in soccer.

99

On his robust tackle on Maurizio Gaudino in a charity football match, May 2006

66

I didn't see it, but it sounds barbaric. It's become like cock-fighting: poor dumb brutes being set upon each other by conniving television producers.

99

On Big Brother, The Observer, *20 June 2004*

"
The only reason I wouldn't visit some parts of New York is the real risk of meeting Donald Trump. **"**

On the Special Relationship,
8 December 2015

66

Virtually every single one of our international sports was invented or codified by the British. And I say this respectfully to our Chinese hosts, who have excelled so magnificently at Ping-pong. Ping-pong was invented on the dining tables of England in the 19th century and it was called Wiff-waff!

99

On British sporting heritage, Olympic flag handover ceremony, August 2008

66

AI – what will it mean? Helpful
robots washing and caring for an
ageing population? Or pink-eyed
terminators sent back from the
future to cull the human race? 99

On artificial intelligence,
UN General Assembly, 25 September 2019

66

The Americans were perfectly happy to go ahead and whack Saddam merely on the grounds that he was a bad guy, and that Iraq and the world would be better off without him; and so indeed was I.

99

On the Iraq War, Daily Telegraph,
5 June 2003

66

Venice, with all her civilisation and ancient beauty, Venice with her addiction to curious aquatic means of transport, yes, my friends, Venice is the Henley of the South.

99

On Venice, Daily Telegraph, *11 March 2004*

"

I'd like thousands of schools
as good as the one I went to,
Eton.

"

On school, GQ magazine, July 2007

CHAPTER
FIVE

BORIS ON BREXIT

66

First they make us pay in our taxes for Greek olive groves, many of which probably don't exist. Then they say we can't dip our bread in olive oil in restaurants. We didn't join the Common Market – betraying the New Zealanders and their butter – in order to be told when, where and how we must eat the olive oil we have been forced to subsidise.

99

On the EU, 28 November 2013

66

Britain is a great nation, a global force for good. It is surely a boon for the world and for Europe that she should be intimately engaged in the EU.

99

Draft of a pre-Brexit referendum, pro-EU column, 2016

Napoleon, Hitler, various people tried this out, and it ends tragically. The EU is an attempt to do this by different methods.

On the European Union,
Sunday Telegraph, *15 May 2016*

There is only one way to get the change we need – and that is to vote to go; because all EU history shows that they only really listen to a population when it says no.

On the need to vote 'Leave',
Daily Telegraph, *16 March 2016*

"

I think the best thing we can do is show a lead, show an example and strike out for freedom.

"

On setting an example for Europe,
11 March 2016

66

They want us to go to the
polls in such a state of quivering
apprehension that we do the
bidding of the Euro-elites,
and vote to stay in the
European Union.

99

On the EU, Daily Telegraph,
28 February 2016

66

This EU referendum has been the most extraordinary political event of our lifetime.

99

On the referendum result,
Daily Telegraph, *26 June 2016*

"

It is said that those who voted Leave were mainly driven by anxieties about immigration. I do not believe that is so.

On the reasons for Brexit,
Daily Telegraph, *26 June 2016*

"

"

Leaving the EU would be a win-win for all. The EU costs us a huge amount of money and subverts our democracy.

"

On the benefits of Brexit, 11 March 2016

> **"**
> After we liberate ourselves from the shackles of Brussels we will be able to create hundreds of thousands of new jobs right across the UK. **"**

On post-Brexit fortunes, 12 May 2016

66

Would anyone in their right mind
want to join the EU today?

99

On the EU, 11 March 2016

"

Take back control of huge sums of money, £350 million a week, and spend it on our priorities such as the NHS.

"

On Brexit priorities, ITV debate, 9 June 2016

“

There is no need for haste about severing the UK's ties [with the EU].

”

On triggering Article 50, 24 June 2016

"

It is vital now to see this moment for what it is. This is not a time to quail, it is not a crisis, nor should we see it as an excuse for wobbling or self-doubt, but it is a moment for hope and ambition for Britain.

"

On making the most of Brexit,
30 June 2016

"
The verdict of history will be that the British people got it right. **"**

On the referendum's legacy,
Daily Telegraph, *26 June 2016*

If Hollande wants to administer punishment beatings to anybody who seeks to escape [the EU], in the manner of some World War Two movie, I don't think that is the way forward, and it's not in the interests of our friends and partners.

On the European response to Brexit, 18 January 2017

66

There is no plan for no deal because we are going to get a great deal.

99

On Brexit negotiations, July 2017

"

The dream is dying, suffocated by needless self-doubt.

"

*On the government's handling of
Brexit, Foreign Secretary resignation letter
9 July 2018*

It is a humiliation. We look like a seven-stone weakling being comically bent out of shape by a 500lb gorilla.

On Theresa May's 'Chequers Plan' for Brexit, Mail on Sunday, *8 September 2018*

[There has been a] collective failure of government, and a collapse of will by the British establishment, to deliver on the mandate of the people.

On the government's handling of Brexit, Daily Telegraph, *27 September 2018*

66

If we get it wrong we will
be punished.

99

Tory Fringe speech on Brexit,
Conservative Party Conference,
2 October 2018

> **“**
>
> Fuck business.
>
> **”**
>
> *When asked about business concerns regarding Brexit, 25 June 2018*

"

[I] didn't say anything about Turkey during the referendum. Since I made no remarks… I can't disown them.

On his conduct during the referendum, 18 January 2019

"

" I'd rather be dead in a ditch. **"**

On whether he'd ask the EU to extend Brexit beyond 31 October 2019, 5 September 2019

"

There's a terrible kind of collaboration as it were, going on between people who think they can block Brexit in Parliament and our European friends.

"

On Parliament's Brexit interventions,
14 August 2019

66

Under no circumstances would we agree to any free-trade deal that put the NHS on the table. 99

On American trade negotiations, 25 July 2019

We are once again going to believe in ourselves, and like some slumbering giant we are going to rise and ping off the guy ropes of self-doubt and negativity.

On positive thinking, Conservative Party Leadership victory speech, 23 July 2019

"

We are going to energise the country. We are going to get Brexit done on 31 October and take advantage of all the opportunities it will bring with a new spirit of can do.

"

On his priority as Prime Minister,
Conservative Party Leadership victory speech,
23 July 2019

" If you Brexit sensibly and effectively, you take away so much of the ammunition of the SNP. **"**

On Scottish independence, 27 June 2019

"

We need to realise the depth of the problems we face. Unless we get on and do this thing, we will be punished for a very long time. There is a very real choice between getting Brexit done and the potential extinction of this great party.

"

On Conservative prospects, 4 June 2019

66

The British people won't be scared into backing a woeful Brexit deal nobody voted for.

On Theresa May's Brexit deal,
The Telegraph, 6 January 2019

99

"

When Prometheus brought fire to mankind… Zeus punished him by chaining him to a Tartarean crag while his liver was pecked out by an eagle. And every time his liver regrew the eagle came back and pecked it again. And this went on forever – a bit like the experience of Brexit in the UK…

"

On Brexit pain, UN General Assembly, 25 September 2019

CHAPTER
SIX

GAFFES
& JIBES

66

[I will lie] in front of those bulldozers and stop the building, stop the construction of that third runway.

99

On the prospect of the third runway at Heathrow, May 2015

66

You throw a stone in Kensington and you'll hit an oligarch, some of them are close to Putin and some of them aren't.

99

On London's Russian population, 24 May 2018

66

What's my view on drugs? I've forgotten my view on drugs.

99

On the campaign trail, 2005

" Here we are in one of the most depressed towns in southern England, a place that is arguably too full of drugs, obesity, underachievement and Labour MPs. **"**

On Portsmouth, GQ magazine, April 2007

66

I can't sit down and negotiate with you on air when you're holding a gun to Londoners' heads and threatening disruption to the greatest city on earth.

99

In conversation with Bob Crow on the London Underground strikes, LBC, 4 February 2014

"

You know, £60 million I saw
was being spaffed up a wall,
you know, on some investigation
into historic child abuse. What
on earth is that going to do to
protect the public now?

"

*On investigating historic sex abuse
cases, LBC, 13 March 2019*

66

Men are said to have differently shaped tear ducts, for instance, and can therefore retain the tears for longer before they splash down the cheek.

99

On why women supposedly cry more often, Daily Telegraph, *14 June 2015*

> **"**
> Unfortunately, some linkside don at a provincial university spotted that by the time the Rose Palace was built, Piers Gaveston would long have been murdered. **"**

On the fabricated story that had him fired from The Times, The Independent, *21 May 2002*

A truly shameful vignette of almost superhuman undergraduate arrogance, toffishness and twittishness.

On the Bullingdon Club, BBC, 19 March 2013

66

I have more in common with a three-toed sloth or a one-eyed pterodactyl or a Kalamata olive than I have with Winston Churchill.

99

On how he matches up to Churchill, 2014

66

Intelligence is really all about energy. You can have the brightest people in the world who simply can't be arsed. No good to man or beast.

99

On the importance of energy, 2003

66

Oh my God, arr, you, you mean
apart from Pericles of Athens?

99

*Responding to Will Smith, when asked
who were his biggest inspirations, 2013*

66

There comes a point when you've got to put the dynamite under your own tram tracks... [and] derail yourself.

On taking risks, Conservative Party magazine, 2001

99

"

You can't rule out the possibility that beneath the elaborately constructed veneer of a blithering idiot, there lurks an, er, blithering idiot.

"

On his hidden depths, Top Gear, 2010

"

[He has shown] a quite stupefying ignorance that makes him, frankly, unfit to hold the office of President of the United States.

"

Responding to Donald Trump's comments on 'no-go zones' in London, 9 December 2015

Sometimes I can think of so many ways of expressing myself that I feel I'm an old typewriter and too many keys come forward at once – and I get jammed.

On expressing himself,
The Spectator, *13 December 2014*

66

I'm made up of immigrant stock, I went to a primary school in London, I grew up eating Spangles, why shouldn't I be as well placed to speak for Londoners as anyone else?

99

On his Londoner credentials,
Time Out, *15 April 2008*

66

Great, supine, protoplasmic
invertebrate jellies!

99

*On opposition members of the London
Assembly, 25 February 2013*

"

Why on earth can it not produce something that is quite as brilliant as *Breaking Bad*?

"

On the BBC, Sky News, 2015

> 66

It would be a sad day if we British stopped being cynical, but you sometimes wonder whether we overdo it.

99

On the British disposition,
Daily Telegraph, *15 December 2014*

I want you to know that I have nothing against Orlando, though you are, of course, far more likely to get shot or robbed there than in London.

On Florida, Daily Telegraph,
7 June 2010

66

I lead a life of blameless domesticity and always have done.

On his private life, GQ magazine, 21 February 2016

99

66

How does it hurt me, with my 20-year-old Toyota, if somebody else has a swish Mercedes? We both get stuck in the same traffic.

99

On inequality, Daily Telegraph, 17 November 2013

66

Am I an invention? I think the truth is, if I tried to be anybody else, you'd be even more dubious.

99

On his character, The Spectator,
13 December 2014

66

I love swimming in rivers, and well remember once jumping in at Chiswick.

99

On swimming, Daily Telegraph, *2 July 2012*

66 That was very bleak. Not very
uplifting. Can't we get a bit of
sunshine in there? **99**

On an unspectacular interview,
Time Out, *15 April 2008*

"

I've never heard such humbug in all my life.

"

*Responding to Labour MP
Paula Sherriff's call to tone down his
inflammatory language,
25 September 2019*